Dehydrating Foods

The Complete Guide to Drying Food.

The Ultimate Food Dehydrator Recipes Cookbook

Dr I. Pot

2

COPYRIGHT

TABLE OF CONTENTS

INTRODUCTION

Food dehydrators extend in cost from about $50 for fundamental machines to well over $300 for better quality purchaser models. It's a great deal of cash for a kitchen apparatus that isn't as vital to food planning as, state, and a blender. Be that as it may, a food dehydrator can give you some new and scrumptious choices for keeping up a sound eating regimen. It can likewise give you another approach to safeguard the great food you have today for some other time. In this book, we investigate a few reasons that a food dehydrator may bode well for you.

A dehydrator strengthens solid food decisions

You're not going to get dried out a cheeseburger, correct? No. When you purchase a dehydrator, you're making a guarantee to solid food. You will dry things like peaches, fruits, apples, bananas, pineapples, and mangos. Perhaps peppers, tomatoes, or kale. These are on the whole nourishments that the vast majority don't get enough of as of now. A dehydrator helps keep quality, sound food at the focal point of your eating routine. That, however a dehydrator expands the solid food you have today into your future, since it permits you to protect great food now for some other time. Ensure you look at our rundown of plans.

A dehydrator gives you new crude food choices

If you're on crude food diet, or simply attempting to eat increasingly crude nourishments, a dehydrator gives you another approach to get ready crude food. A decent dehydrator has a flexible indoor regulator and can keep up an even temperature at or under 115 F. A great deal of dehydrator plans and guidelines will call for drying foods grown from the ground in the 130-140 F go, however lessening the temperature works fine if you simply broaden the drying time. A dehydrator can likewise be utilized to heat up soups and sauces at low temperatures, and to make crude wafers, breads, granolas, and treats.

A dehydrator permits you to purchase quality at a lower cost

See a few organic products or vegetables on special that you don't require a few seconds ago? A dehydrator permits you to purchase additional food now and dry it for some other time. Natural products like bananas, mangos, strawberries, and fruits often go on special when they become completely ready. A dehydrator gives you an approach to purchase more than you need right now at a bargain, and dry it for some other time. For instance, you may purchase an instance of ready peaches, then make a peach pie utilizing a portion of the peaches, and dry the rest into scrumptious peach wedges.

You can make your own lightweight outdoors food

If you do any hiking or any outdoors where low weight is significant, a dehydrator is an approach to make scrumptious and light food. When nourishments are dried out, the greater part of the water is expelled, which additionally evacuates the majority of the weight. In any event, something massive and substantial, similar to a watermelon, can be dried into "chips" that can be hurled into a sandwich sack. Additionally, a dehydrator gives an approach to make progressively confounded nourishments, similar to spaghetti, versatile. You can make astounding spaghetti sauce or stew (with or without meat) that will taste similarly as great on the path as it did at home. If you're eager and have the correct fire or oven, you can make an extraordinary pizza or calzone with a dried out tomato sauce and dried vegetables.

A great venture with the children

Getting ready nourishment for drying is a great task for the children. Ordinarily, the food you are drying should be washed, cut into cuts, and orchestrated pleasantly on plate. Children love washing and masterminding, and they particularly like undertakings where there is an award toward the end. Many dried organic products taste practically like taffy - an incredible trade for sweets or lousy nourishment. Practically all natural product cowhide will be mainstream with your children, yet additionally attempt bananas, strawberries, kiwis, mangos, pineapples, and even watermelon or melon. When your children request dried natural product as though it were sweets, you'll realize it was justified, despite all the trouble.

You can have a greater nursery

Love to cultivate yet make some hard memories dealing with all the food that your nursery produces? A dehydrator gives you an incredible method to safeguard certain nourishments for some other time. With a dehydrator, you can get great outcomes with carrots, corn, parsley, tomatoes, peppers, peas, garlic, and even horseradish. Only rehydrate before utilizing in soups, stews, or to cook legitimately. You can likewise make vegetable pieces and powders to use in soups, sauces, servings of mixed greens, and seasonings.

You can dry your own herbs

A dehydrator is the most effective and flavor-safeguarding approach to dry herbs that look and taste incredible. With an even, controlled temperature of 90-105 F, you can regularly dry herbs in 1 to 3 hours. Dry your own basil, mustard, mint, ginger, dill, thyme, and rosemary.

You can supplant numerous costly snacks with your own dried food

A dehydrator gives you an extraordinary method to supplant numerous costly snacks with more beneficial food you make yourself. An enormous number of generally accessible organic products make an extraordinary in a hurry nibble for work, game, or play. Have a go at drying out apricots, peaches, apples, pineapple, bananas, blueberries, strawberries, kiwi, plums, pears, and grapes. You can likewise make brilliant progressively complete bites by joining natural product cowhides with other solid fixings. Rather than purchasing an instance of intensity bars marked down for $20.00, make your own organic product calfskin sprinkled and moved with nuts, seeds, or granola.

You can make your own meat jerky

For some individuals, jerky is the principle reason they own a dehydrator. Jerky is a lean and tasty wellspring of protein; extraordinary as a base for a light lunch or to take with you when climbing, working outside, or in any event. Locally acquired jerky is costly and doesn't taste on a par with the jerky you can make yourself. A dehydrator permits you make magnificent meat, fish, and even turkey jerky. There are countless pre-blended jerky flavors accessible, and you can make your own to taste.

Dehydrators are an astounding method to safeguard food

The even warmth of a food dehydrator makes food that is healthfully better than canned food. When put away appropriately, dried nourishments stay sound and nutritious for a considerable length of time or months at room temperature and by and large longer than a year in a cooler. Also, no synthetic concoctions or additives are required.

Constrained distinctly by your creative mind, the advanced food dehydrator has been intended to dry a various scope of products of the soil by managing the temperature for even and steady drying. These helpful kitchen machines are rapidly turning into a family unit staple over the UK as they are anything but difficult to utilize, economical to run and offer a sound choice to locally acquired merchandise.

1. Got dried out Foods Taste Great

Utilizing a food dehydrator to expel dampness from food, for example, organic products, vegetables, and meats makes normally focused, rich, and scrumptious tasting food.

That, yet when making food yourself, you know the quality and newness of the produce you are utilizing - dissimilar to when eating got dried out nourishments bought from the supermarket.

2. Diminish food squander and expand timeframe of realistic usability

Never squander food again with a food dehydrator. Utilizing your extra products of the soil in a food dehydrator will expand their timeframe of realistic usability for as long as 2 years! Truly, it's hard to believe, but it's true - 2 years!

The following are only a couple of ways you can lessen food squander by protecting food with a dehydrator and keeping your wash room supplied all year while setting aside yourself some cash all the while;

Deal with a greater veggie or herb garden without the concern of food going to squander - essentially utilize the dehydrator to dry your herbs or make veggie chips. A few veggies that work extraordinary in the dehydrator incorporate kale, beetroot, turnips, carrots, yams and even green beans.

Purchase mass in season to set aside your family cash. For instance; purchase a plate of mangoes in summer, get dried out them and be having new mango smoothies in winter!

Spare nourishments that would somehow or another ruin, similar to the overlooked natural product in the rear of your fridge, and transform them into scrumptious solid treats and bites like organic product cowhides.

Dried out food can be likewise be "re-hydrated" essentially with water or by adding to soups, meals, stews or pasta sauces.

3. Make Healthy and 100% Natural Foods

Drying out nourishments requires just a single fixing, the food you're drying, so in addition to the fact that it is 100% regular, however you profit by all the minerals and fiber of the entire natural product, and dissimilar to cooking and steaming, you don't lose any of the dietary substance of the food sources you are getting dried out.

Drying out will change the manner in which you take a gander at nourishments. Straightforward products of the soil can be changed into delectable, sound bites and treats. Sound choices to lousy nourishments can be made in a dehydrator and the conceivable outcomes are actually huge! You will likely be amazed at the measure of nourishments which you devour which are really dried and you can make yourself - sultanas, dried herbs, dates and so on.

Got dried out Mango

When we consider dried organic product, we will in general partner it with a "solid tidbit" and a great deal of when individuals are eating fewer carbs they devour huge amounts of dried natural product thinking it is a sound option in contrast to desserts or lollies. Be that as it may, this isn't the situation when it comes to locally acquired dried natural product. Many locally acquired dried organic products contain included sugars, sulfur dioxide and trans fat - which can all be destructive to you and your family!

Sulfur dioxide is now and again added to locally acquired dried organic product so as to forestall discoloration. Sulfur dioxide can cause asthma, skin rashes and stomach torments. Sulfur dioxide is especially present in dried apricots, which is the thing that gives them the splendid orange shading.

By making your own dried organic products, there is no an added substance or additives - you are in charge of what goes into your food! If you are sick of not having the option to give your kids and family sound tidbits, a food dehydrator is your answer.

4. Cost Savings

Prepared, locally acquired tidbits can be costly and natural dried out nourishments are often profoundly over estimated. You can set aside a great deal of cash by utilizing your own food dehydrator and by buying new food things in mass when in season, or by collecting your own produce.

However food dehydrators are incredibly practical to run. For instance, the 6 Tray BioChef Arizona Dehydrator costs only $0.84 to run over 8 hour duration - the normal drying time required for natural product or veggie chips.

Along these lines, exploit those arrangements from your nearby supermarket or rancher's market and make sure to dry out your nourishments and store them for some other time.

5. Proficient Storing

Dried nourishments take short of what one 6th of their unique extra room and don't require the progressing electrical channel of a fridge or cooler. Essentially pack the nourishments spotless, dry, creepy crawly verification compartments or canning containers, plastic cooler holders with tight fitting tops, plastic cooler sacks or vacuum seal sacks (in single part sizes) and store them in your wash room for the ideal go-to nibble.

This significant decrease in size implies that you can fit a great deal of jelly into a little territory - which is particularly perfect for outdoors, trekking and huge families.

6. Conveyability

Got dried out nourishments are conservative, lightweight and they travel well.

As featured before, sound nourishments and tidbits can be costly and you can't generally discover, or approach them in a hurry. By getting dried out nourishments at home, you can make the ideal nibble for your youngsters' school lunch boxes or a late morning hunger-buster for while you're out and about or at work.

7. Exactness Drying

If you've at any point attempted to dry out nourishments in your broiler then you'll comprehend the dissatisfaction it can at times cause - not just because of the higher power costs that you'll need to pay, but since most family stoves don't begin their temperature measures underneath 90 degrees (Celsius)! Conversely, by utilizing a food dehydrator, you have unlimited oversight when drying nourishments at lower temperatures. For instance; the BioChef Arizona Dehydrator offers a flexible indoor regulator scope of 35 - 70 degrees Celsius - significantly lower than your normal family broiler.

Because of these low temperatures, food made with a dehydrator is often considered as 'crude food'. A crude food diet has numerous advantages, and is said to safeguard the living supplements and chemicals in products of the soil not at all like the warming procedure which is said to take out or drain these from food.

Thusly, if you're on a crude food diet, or are simply attempting to eat progressively crude nourishments, a dehydrator gives a decent option in contrast to getting ready nourishments at a temperature underneath 46 degrees Celsius - the limit temperature where catalysts and supplements are viewed as kept up - than some other kitchen machine available.

8. Adaptable and Versatile

Regardless of whether you need to make organic product cowhides, enact a few nuts or make a clump of veggie chips, food dehydrators give you the adaptability to do every last bit of it - in addition to you have the choice to run the machine for a time of hours, or over various days!

While you are just constrained by your creative mind, beneath are only a couple of the things you can make with a food dehydrator...

Got dried out Fruit Roll Ups - these are a champ with the children! Basically mix products of the soil (some yogurt) get dried out and move up. It's the ideal lunchbox nibble.

Dried organic products, for example, grapes, blueberries, strawberries, mangoes, bananas, pineapple and kiwi are natural product.

Solid vegetable chips - make firm chips from beetroot, carrot, parsnip and yam with no oil

Jerky - try different things with different assortments: meat, sheep, fish and poultry with additive free, new marinades and flavors

Make sound bread choices, for example, flax seed bread, pizza bases and wafers

Solid granola, actuated nuts and seeds

Sound pooch and creature treats without additives

Dried Chips

For additional thoughts, tips and deceives, or for more food dehydrator plans look at our food dehydrator formula segment here.

9. Straightforward and Easy to Use

So straightforward and simple to utilize, food dehydrators are basically idiot proof! With the clear set and overlook framework, you just set up your food by cutting into pieces, pop onto the plate, set a clock and leave. It's that simple!

Also, you'll be excited to realize that the temperatures are set so low that it's practically difficult to over dry your nourishments, and if you do, you can generally 're-hydrate' them with a little water or by adding them to soups, goulashes, stews or pasta sauces.

10. Safe Preservation - Very generally safe of microscopic organisms and ruining

In contrast to other protection strategies, because food dehydrators expel the water content from nourishments during the drying procedure, the danger of microscopic organisms' development or ruining is exceptionally low. Truth be told, lack of hydration is ordinarily utilized by campers, climbers and even space explorers because of the sheltered idea of the protection technique!

Imperativeness 4 Life have painstakingly chosen and structured a scope of food dehydrators, each with their own highlights, to make the getting dried out procedure basic and simple.

WHAT IS DEHYDRATING?

Dehydration is a condition that outcomes when the body loses more water than it take in. This lopsidedness upsets the typical degrees of salts and sugars present in the blood, which can meddle with the manner in which the body capacities.

66% of the human body is made out of water, which helps in various capacities, for example, grease of the joints and eyes, assimilation, and the flushing out of squanders and poisons. As the water content in the blood starts to decay, the subsequent unevenness in the degrees of minerals, salts and sugars can cause a few hurtful impacts.

Side effects and indications of dehydration

A portion of the early indications of dehydration include:

Exceptional thirst

Feeling discombobulated or bleary eyed

Having concentrated pee that is dull in shading and solid in smell

A decrease in the recurrence of pee

In babies, signs remember the weakness for the highest point of the skull (fontanelle) being depressed; few or no tears shed on crying, less wet nappies, and sleepiness.

Reasons for dehydration

Dehydration is typically brought about by an insufficient admission of liquids to supplant those that have been lost. Other contributing components incorporate atmosphere, physical action and diet. Dehydration is likewise brought about by sicknesses that may prompt liquid misfortune, for example, industrious looseness of the bowels and spewing.

Wearable sensors decipher dynamic perspiration piece

Children and newborn children are at the most serious danger of turning out to be got dried out because their low body weight makes them delicate to even a minor loss of liquid. The older are additionally at a more serious hazard because they might be less aware of dehydration setting in and not understand they have to drink liquids. Individuals who are diabetic or who experience the ill effects of liquor abuse are likewise at a more serious danger of dehydration and competitors can be influenced because of the measure of body liquid lost through perspiration.

Treatment

An individual who is dried out necessities to drink a lot of liquids, for example, water, squash or natural product juice, however ought to stay away from stimulated refreshments and bubbly beverages.

If diseases, for example, heaving or looseness of the bowels are making it difficult to hold water down, little tastes ought to be tanked. Babies and kids who are dried out ought not to be given water as this can weaken the effectively low degrees of electrolytes and minerals in the body. The World Health Organization suggests the utilization of oral rehydration arrangements, which are particularly intended for kids with looseness of the bowels and dehydration. The arrangement contains a blend of potassium, salts and sugars to reestablish the right equalization of body liquids.

Brief treatment of dehydration is significant, as extreme dehydration can cause life-undermining difficulties and even passing.

During looseness of the bowels there is an expanded loss of water and electrolytes (sodium, chloride, potassium, and bicarbonate) in the fluid stool. Water and electrolytes are additionally lost through regurgitation, sweat, and pee and relaxing. Dehydration happens when these misfortunes are not supplanted enough and a deficiency of water and electrolytes creates.

The volume of liquid lost through the stools in 24 hours can shift from 5 ml/kg (close to typical) to 200 ml/kg, or more. The fixations and measures of electrolytes lost likewise differ. The all out body sodium deficiency in small kids with serious dehydration because of loose bowels is ordinarily around 70110 mill moles per liter of water shortfall. Potassium and chloride misfortunes are in a comparable range. Deficiencies of this extent can happen with intense looseness of the bowels of any etiology. The most well-known reasons for dehydration are rotavirus, enterotoxigenic Escherichia coli (ETEC) and, during plagues, Vibrio cholerae O1 or O139.

The level of dehydration is evaluated by signs and manifestations that mirror the measure of liquid lost:

In the beginning periods of dehydration, there are no signs or side effects.

As dehydration expands, signs and manifestations create. These include: thirst, eager or touchy conduct, diminished skin turgor, dry mucous films, indented eyes, depressed fontanelle (in newborn children), and nonappearance of tears when crying overwhelmingly.

In serious dehydration, these impacts become increasingly articulated and the patient may create proof of hypovolaemic stun, including: reduced awareness, absence of pee yield, cool wet furthest points, a quick and weak heartbeat (the outspread heartbeat might be imperceptible), low or imperceptible pulse, and fringe cyanosis.

Demise follows soon if rehydration isn't begun rapidly. Dehydration is the loss of water and body salts through loose bowels. The human body needs water to keep up enough blood and different liquids to work appropriately. If your body loses considerably a greater number of liquids than you are drinking, you become got dried out. You may lose liquids in an assortment of ways:

when peeing

when you upchuck or have the runs

when perspiring

from the lungs during ordinary relaxing.

Alongside the liquids, your body likewise loses electrolytes, which are salts regularly found in blood, different liquids, and cells.

BENEFITS OF DEHYDRATING

Making your own dried out food has a great deal of advantages. If you utilize your food dehydrator routinely, it can offer you reserve funds, medical advantages and a greener lifestyle. If you're considering purchasing a food dehydrator, you ought to know about the advantages and nuts and bolts of making your own dried out food.

1. Tastes Great

Got dried out food is simply food–generally natural product, vegetables or meat–with the entirety of the dampness dried out of it. Without the dampness to water down the taste, the food is rich and flavorful. That, however the food is likewise new when you make it yourself. Making it yourself permits you to appreciate this newness, not at all like you would if you ate the dried out food sold at the market.

2. More affordable

Handled bites cost a considerable amount of cash all alone, and solid and natural dried out food cost much more. You can set aside a great deal of cash by purchasing new food in mass and getting dried out it yourself. That way you can exploit any arrangements you find at your supermarket's produce segment by getting dried out it and putting away it for some other time. This training will likewise permit you to supplant many locally acquired bites. The entirety of this includes, and you will find that you are spending significantly less over the long haul.

3. All Natural

When you purchase got dried out food or different tidbits, you don't generally have a clue what's in it. There are numerous added substances and additives put in handled nourishments. These additives expand the time span of usability of the food and will commonly modify the nature taste of the food.

Sugar is often added to dried out natural product; in any case, when you make it yourself in your food dehydrator, you are in charge of what is and isn't included. You won't need to peruse the fixing list on bundles and stress over how those unpronounceable synthetic substances are influencing your body. Rather, you can just dry your own new fixings and have a nibble for the street.

4. Compact

It very well may be difficult to track down sound food that you can take in a hurry. Beside bananas, there isn't a lot of that is anything but difficult to eat and won't make a wreck. It is likewise particularly hazardous to eat while you're attempting to drive. With your got dried out food, you can simply have a plastic pack on your lap brimming with your bite. It's extraordinary for youngsters' snacks at school or a late morning nibble at work, as well.

5. Decreases Waste

In the U.S. alone, we some way or another figure out how to squander $165 billion worth of food consistently. With a dehydrator, you can lessen squander by getting dried out nourishments that are verging on ruining. When your new natural product begins going delicate, cut it up and put it in the food dehydrators. If you have meat that should be cooked, make some jerky. This technique can help you from tossing out that sack of apples or pack of bananas that you overlooked until they began turning earthy colored. Essentially cut them up and appreciate them later!

Points of interest of Using a Food Dehydrator

If you are keen on drying out your nourishments yet don't have the suggested gear, realize that it is conceivable to utilize the broiler to dry out the nourishments utilizing low temperatures for extensive stretches of time. Be that as it may, there are numerous favorable circumstances to utilizing a dehydrator rather than a broiler. For one, the food will have any longer time span of usability if you utilize a legitimate food dehydrator. The dehydrator will expel all the dampness from the food appropriately, and your food will really have the option to be put away around one year longer than if you utilized a stove rather, if kept in legitimate conditions.

Dehydrators are additionally simple on your wallet. While there is a forthright cost, they wind up paying for themselves a few times over if utilized oftentimes. These are little machines that utilization almost no power. They likewise set aside you cash because they keep you from expecting to warm a whole stove to get dried out your food. You just need to warm the little space which spares you vitality just as opens up your broiler if you need it for something different.

Instructions to Dehydrate Food

The right food dehydration technique relies upon what you are drying out. The vast majority of the nourishments don't generally require any readiness. In any case, it is suggested that you ensure your vegetables look whitened before placing them in the dehydrator. Whitening vegetables will cause them to get dried out more rapidly and will likewise set the shading so they don't look blurred and unwanted once they're done. When it comes to really getting dried out, you ought to consistently follow the headings for the specific food dehydrator that you have.

Dehydrator Choices

If you don't have a dehydrator yet, there are some incredible ones out there to pick from. You can purchase a dehydrator for as meager as $50 and as much as a few hundred. Here are some incredible decisions.

1. Nesco American Harvest 400W Food Dehydrator

This dehydrator is the ideal modest alternative for somebody who is simply starting to dry out their food. Not exclusively would you be able to utilize this dehydrator to make delightful veggie and organic product chips, yet it can likewise be utilized to make jerky. Because of its weight and size–5 lbs. furthermore, 14.1″ H x 9.2″ W x 14.2″ D–this dehydrator can be effectively moved and put away in any kitchen.

The Nesco American Harvest Food Dehydrator touts its licensed fan stream outspread air drying innovation, which guarantees that your food will dry uniformly. This implies you don't have to turn your food during the drying procedure. The four plates permit you to dry a ton of veggie chips or jerky at once.

2. Koolatron Total Chef 5 Tray Food Dehydrator

Another less expensive yet very compelling choice of food dehydrator is the Koolatron Total Chef 5 Tray Dehydrator. You can move up to this Koolatron dehydrator for just about $80. This dehydrator has a bigger number of alternatives than different dehydrators, including five removable plates and a convection warming framework.

This food dehydrator is useful for anything you desire to get dried out, including organic products, vegetables and meats. The unmistakable plate makes it simpler for you to screen your nourishments as they dry. The smaller size–8" H x 13" W x 13" L–makes this machine simple for anybody to utilize and store.

3. Excalibur 9 Tray Food Dehydrator with Timer

This is an incredible dehydrator for somebody who has focused on the great propensity for drying out nourishments, however perhaps less for the learners. If the reasonable dehydrators aren't sufficient for you, you can purchase an Excalibur dehydrator–however it will interfere with you two or three hundred dollars.

This dehydrator highlights nine plates, permitting you to dry out a ton of food on the double. You can spread out a lot of jerky or make enough dried organic product for the entire family in only one use. What makes the Excalibur dehydrator so effective is that it utilizes a flat wind current drying framework as opposed to transmitting heat all through the unit. This guarantees each plate gets a similar measure of warming and drying power.

4. Nesco Snackmaster Express Food Dehydrator All-In-One Kit

This Nesco Snackmaster Express Food Dehydrator is a top merchant for Nesco. It has four plates, like the American Harvest food dehydrator recorded previously. The difference is that this dehydrator can really be extended if you have to get dried out multiple plate worth of food at once.

The dehydrator works equitably, so you don't have to turn plate like you would with more affordable items, and it has a temperature scope of 95° F – 155° F. The structure likewise makes it simple to utilize and simple to clean. Probably the best thing about this dehydrator is that it works quick as opposed to sitting tight a few days for your food to completely get dried out, you can make the most of your food in only a couple of brief hours.

Long haul Benefits

Getting dried out food is a decent propensity to embrace because it can profit your wellbeing and your wallet rather rapidly. With the a wide range of sorts of food dehydrators accessible today, it ought not be too difficult to even consider finding one that isn't excessively costly however can at present take care of business to your gauges.

You've more than likely heard some buzz about food drying out, however perhaps you don't totally comprehend what it's everything about. Or then again perhaps you've never attempted it yourself.

In any case, I'm here to assist you with bettering comprehend the advantages of getting dried out food because if you aren't as of now doing it, you're truly passing up a great opportunity!

There are numerous surprising reasons drying food can be stunning for your wellbeing, your spending plan, and your life. Along these lines, how about we make a plunge and discussion about them!

Here are the top advantages of food drying out and why it's an extraordinary procedure to add to your life:

1. Nutritious and Healthy for You

A food dehydrator benefits you by holding the first nutrients, minerals, and common catalysts of nourishments obviously better than different types of food conservation or cooking. Actually, an examination in Journal of the American College of Nutrition in 2005 indicated dried organic products like dried cranberries, grapes, and plums had double the measure of cancer prevention agents as their new forms!

This is significant in our cutting edge world where we're encircled by bundled and synthetically adjusted nourishments with next to no nutritive worth.

In addition, most sound nourishments aren't accessible all year (or they don't taste as great and are progressively costly when not in-season), so drying out them to appreciate whenever is an extraordinary method to keep up assortment while eating well consistently.

What's more the medical advantages of food dehydration, did I notice there are TONS of delectable choices to look over? Instances of nourishments you can make in a dehydrator include:

Dried natural product tidbits or chips from apples, bananas, oranges, pears, prunes, or lemons

Veggie chips from zucchini, kale, carrots, green beans, or yams (here's an extraordinary guide for getting dried out vegetables)

Jerky from meat, salmon, chicken, or sheep

Natural product cowhides produced using pureed dried organic products (essentially like the natural product rendition of hamburger jerky)

Sun-dried (got dried out) tomatoes

Granola and fresh nuts and seeds

Crude saltines or breads

Full suppers that can be rehydrated later

Dried herbs and blossoms

Thus significantly more!

Feel free to investigate with these simple and solid dehydrator plans.

2. No Preservatives or Chemicals

Got dried out food contains just a single fixing: the food you're drying out. No compelling reason to stress over extra troublesome synthetic compounds or fixings you can't articulate being added to it.

Not just that, home-dried out products of the soil can be useful for a considerable length of time—often up to an entire year! What's more, locally acquired got dried out nourishments can last many, numerous years.

3. Sets aside You Cash

We could all utilization more approaches to set aside cash, correct? All things considered, envision purchasing mass produce at a limited rate (at your nearby plantation or supermarket), getting dried out it at home, and having it accessible to eat whenever all consistently.

Think: less additional outings to the market for produce, less utilization of gas, and having "gourmet" nourishments like sun-dried tomatoes or kale chips—with no additional oils, additives, salts, or sugars—for a small amount of the bundled cost.

With getting dried out, the entirety of this is conceivable! The cost-proficiency of food dehydration is truly stunning.

4. Simple Storage and Preservation

Presently, we should talk stockpiling. The advantages of getting dried out nourishment for protection are twofold:

by evacuating the entirety of the food's dampness, you repress the development of microbes so the food remains safeguarded and safe any longer and

you shrivel the size of the food, making stockpiling a snap.

That implies you'll have progressively sound nourishments in your kitchen for a more extended timeframe without stressing over ruining. State adiós to locally acquired bundled nourishments and old, rotten produce!

5. Make an Assortment of Homemade Goods

It's an obvious fact that natively constructed dinners and tidbits are better decisions over their eatery or bundled variants because you can control the fixings that go into them. You can bunch set up your dried out nourishments so you ALWAYS have a weapons store of solid choices to snatch from home.

That is not all, however. A food dehydrator can do numerous different things past simply make got dried out nourishments! You can use for making natively constructed things like:

Dried herbs

Natural teas

Blend and dried blossoms

Fire starters

Pooch treats

Paper (from drying the mash of reused things)

Along these lines, other than improving your wellbeing and setting aside you cash, getting dried out is extraordinary for improving a few parts of your home life, also.

6. Compact

A typical whine about eating well is that it's difficult to do while voyaging. I can comprehend the thinking; however that is the place the advantages of a food dehydrator can spare you from falling back on the drive-through.

Getting dried out gives you sound, non-muddled tidbits prepared to snatch n-go, making them incredibly simple to take with you anyplace—in the vehicle, on a plane, while exploring, or on an outdoors trip, and so on.

Who needs cheap food when you can have nutritious dried organic products, veggies, grains, and a wide range of good nourishments with you whenever?

7. Ideal for Plant-Based Diets

Foods grown from the ground, in abundance! These are clearly staples on a plant-based eating routine. What's more, just from taking a gander at the got dried out food models in #1, you can see most of them are plants.

There are huge amounts of plant-based plans you can make with a food dehydrator, for example, wafers, organic product snacks, crude bread, and veggie lover jerky to give some examples. What's more, with a dehydrator cookbook or other veggie lover cookbook formula controls close by; will undoubtedly prepare an interminable measure of truly scrumptious and solid plant-based food choices.

8. Decreases Waste

How often have you purchased a ton of produce at the store just to acknowledge you can't eat everything before it turns sour or gets excessively ready? I realize it's transpired commonly.

Be that as it may, since drying out expands time span of usability so well, you can dodge ever tossing out additional nourishments and dispense with pointless waste. You'll be taking advantage of food you buy.

9. Sets you up for Emergencies

You know the colloquialism, "you can never be excessively arranged"? From a lost employment to a cataclysmic event, you can never know without a doubt what may occur.

Be that as it may, you do have some power over your degree of crisis readiness. Also, got dried out nourishments are the ideal asset for this since you'll generally approach a less-transient, sound, and very much saved food gracefully.

Other than drying singular nourishments, you can likewise dry out whole suppers for your family so that in the event of a crisis, you should simply add water when prepared to eat.

These nine advantages of getting dried out food show how the procedure causes you eat better, live better, and increment your degrees of readiness and food conservation in a totally different manner. The significance is really life-evolving!

THE BEST ELECTRIC DEHYDRATORS

We should take a gander at how the best dehydrators work and the highlights and advantages of very much structured models.

HOW THEY WORK

Dehydrators are generally little estimated machines that are ideal for drying organic products, vegetables, seeds, herbs, fish and meats.

If you develop your own new vegetables or have delivering natural product trees, grape vines or berry shrubs, you would most likely truly value having the option to put some up without spending important cooler space (or uncovering it – particularly from a chest type).

Or then again you can experience the more work concentrated procedure of canning it which, on account of natural product, for the most part adds more sugar to the finished result.

For those that don't have the advantage of claiming your own nursery, you can exploit occasional contributions by shopping the deals in the produce showcase and profiting by scaled down costs.

Easy to utilize dehydrators come in numerous sizes with differing quantities of racks or plate for drying.

You place the food on a plate and the apparatus gradually appropriates warmed air all through the work secured plate.

The machines produce exceptionally delicate warmth (at any rate the great ones) that dries the food at a moderate and even rate, saving the natural issue and forestalling "case solidifying" outwardly.

Case solidifying happens when the natural products, vegetables, or meats are warmed excessively quick, framing a seal outwardly and catching in dampness.

It is imperative to evacuate however much water as could reasonably be expected in the drying procedure.

Each dehydrator will work a smidgen differently and the rate at which nourishments can be dried will change as needs be.

For instance, thicker, denser nourishments will take more time to dry contrasted with something like delicate organic product, which separates all the more without any problem.

As you work with another machine, you will come to become familiar with the proper sizes to cut different organic products, meats and vegetables to acquire the most effective drying process.

Highlights

Look at all the primary highlights of a dehydrator so you may pick the best item for your motivations. Hope to perceive what number of drying levels or plate accompany the machine.

Consider the normal measure of food you will dry at any one time. Check the area of the warming component to see that fluids won't trickle legitimately onto it.

When contrasting models, attempt to search for items that have at any rate 500 watts of intensity. 1000 is far and away superior.

An inherent clock is a pleasant dehydrator highlight, however not a necessity. I for one want to have a clock since it is conceivable to over dry your food and fundamentally consume it.

With a clock, you can go out, rest, and so forth with the machine despite everything working and you don't need to stress over consumed apple rings when you wake up or return.

Indeed, things may not be dried out the entirety of the way, however it is better than having toasted roma tomatoes (incidentally – that is one of my top choices to get dried out, and they're extraordinary in our formula for Sicilian pasta plate of mixed greens!).

Consider better-structured dehydrators with customizable indoor regulators for drying different sorts of grub. This is another component that I consider non-debatable.

Different nourishments case solidify at different temperatures. Meat can be warmed a lot quicker than most natural product, and meat is something that you need to polish off rapidly to forestall microorganisms and form development.

Having the fan on the top or side keeps beads from hitting the warming components, which can mix different flavors all through the machine. Onion enhanced strawberries don't sound excessively tantalizing.

Consider the size of any machine that you buy with the goal that it tends to be put away in a kitchen cupboard or on the ledge if wanted. I keep mine on the extra "lager" cooler in the carport.

Likewise, you should analyze guarantees and look at client audits on the web

Advantages

You can set up nourishments for getting dried out as often as you like.

If you develop your own foods grown from the ground, you can dry them in season and save them without the requirement for extra electrical force, for example, you would require if they were solidified. In addition, they are as yet safe when if the force goes out.

Drying out your produce is likewise not so work escalated as home canning (despite the fact that I do both consistently). You can likewise protect the time span of usability of numerous sorts of home-dried produce much further, utilizing oxygen safeguards and desiccant bundles.

Climbers and campers can exploit these gadgets to get dried out most loved nourishments for open air exercises. They can pack of a great deal of good calories and nutrients in an extremely little and lightweight bundle that can be rehydrated whenever.

Have a bit (or huge) kid that adores jerky however you don't cherish the expense? Make it for as little as possible! Utilize less expensive and more slender cuts of hamburger and it'll taste better than locally acquired. Need to flavor up a stew or soup? Toss a couple of bunches of dried tomatoes, corn, peppers, and so forth in the blend and it'll put a grin all over. A total stew can really be made with 100% got dried out materials.

MOST ELEVATED RATED FOOD DEHYDRATORS

Also, here are Foodal's present proposals for 8 of the best food dehydrators available (+1 for the magnificent Excalibur model that has just been secured).

NESCO FD-1040 GARDENMASTER

The Nesco FD-1040 Gardenmaster offers some extremely sweet highlights typically just found in more expensive units, and they score huge focuses with the home-drying out specialist.

With 1,000 watts of intensity, Nesco's licensed wind stream framework, and the top mounted warmer and fan, this present model's presentation is well over that of practically identical stackable plate units.

Built of without bpa plastic in the US, it has great quality development at the unobtrusive cost tag. Furthermore, its clock and flexible indoor regulator make activity straightforward, simple and bother free.

With a constrained 1-year guarantee and plastic materials, it's not intended for starting your own locally situated jerky business. Be that as it may, it is perfect for exploiting deals, a little nursery reap, or for making sound bites.

This four-plate stackable model offers incredible incentive for a conservative drier.

Peruse Foodal's itemized survey now or read more client assessments on Amazon.

PRESTO 3601 DEHYDRO

From Presto comes the Dehydro Electric Food Dehydrator, a six plate stackable model with a base mounted warming unit and fan.

Expandable up to 12 plates, the Dehydro likewise incorporates a liberal cluster of frill for making natural product cowhide and for drying littler things, for example, herbs, nuts and flavors.

Presto 06301 Dehydro Digital Electric Food Dehydrator

The 700 watt warmer and fan give the perfect conditions to dry out various nourishments, and the programmable clock and customizable indoor regulator guarantee ideal presentation to the right temperatures.

Simple to utilize and clean, the Presto 3601 Dehydro has discovered an invite specialty in numerous kitchens with its helpful size and prudent sticker price.

A solid dryer at the cost, the Presto client support sparkles too.

Perfect for the individuals who need to dry littler estimated clumps, for intermittent use, or for the individuals who essentially would prefer not to put a ton of cash in a dehydrator.

NESCO SNACKMASTER PRO

The No. 1 Bestseller on Amazon in Dehydrators, the Nesco Snackmaster Pro Food Dehydrator is a straightforward and simple to utilize stackable food dehydrator.

It will effectively dry natural product, veggies, herbs, nuts, berries, and jerky surprisingly fast – ideal for you to appreciate home safeguarded goodness.

Nesco Snackmaster Pro Food Dehydrator FD-75A

Nesco has built up a licensed drying framework called Converga-Flow, which makes vertical and level wind current for quick, even and nutritious drying.

The top mounted fan and radiator dispenses with the chaos of fluid dribbling into the warming chamber, and the 700 watts of intensity give all the vitality expected to the movable indoor regulator.

Ideal for the apprentice, the Snackmaster offers simple, dependable outcomes and the alternative to extend for bigger amounts once you get your procedure under control – it's a smash hit all things considered.

L'EQUIP 528

If you need an all-around manufactured unit that will dry nourishments adequately, and in incredible enough amounts to make it beneficial, then a model, for example, the L'Equip 528 may have an incentive for you.

A first class stackable plate dehydrator, the 528 is reasonable, simple to utilize and accompanies a significant 10-year maker's guarantee.

L'Equipe 528 500-watt 6 Tray Food Dehydrator

Something other than an attractive profile, the L'Equip accompanies 12 square feet of usable drying space on 6 plates, and can be extended as far as possible up to 20 plates.

With a strong state variable temperature control, the L'Equip highlights a microchip controlled warming sensor that continually screens the warmth to give a stable drying condition to uniform outcomes. Furthermore, its smooth and ageless structure is anything but difficult to clean and use, making it an esteemed expansion in any kitchen.

A solid entertainer, it's a decent decision for the individuals who appreciate trustworthy outcomes and the capacity to change cluster sizes.

SMELL PROFESSIONAL 6 TRAYS

It is safe to say that you are hoping to progress from stackable plate food dehydrators to the further developed rack plate models? If along these lines, you might need to consider the Aroma Professional 6 Tray Food Dehydrator.

With a moderate size limit and the unwavering quality of rack plate execution, the Professional offers all the highlights required for exceptional outcomes.

The Aroma Professional 6 Tray Food Dehydrator

It's intended to give uniform and reliably warmed even wind current for trustworthy, dependable outcomes with all fixings

The roomy front mounting plate slide on guides simply like the racks in a standard broiler, and the straightforward entryway gains it simple to check ground as nourishments dry.

What's more, cleanup is simple with the included trickle plate that gathers any juices and buildup during the drying procedure.

Ideal for the home aficionado, explorer, or anybody attempting to be somewhat more wellbeing cognizant, the Aroma Professional is prepared, capable and ready to take on any obligations relegated to it.

STX DEHYDRA 1200W 10 RACK STAINLESS STEEL MODEL

For the genuine food getting dried out lover, the STX Dehydra offers an amazing drying framework with an enormous limit, and is intended to convey both amount and quality.

It offers ideal drying times by means of the variable indoor regulator and 16 square feet of usable drying surface, and the back mounted radiator and fan give abundant wind stream to guarantee legitimate dehydration.

STX INTERNATIONAL Dehydra STX-DEH-1200W-XLS 10-Tray Stainless Steel Digital Food Dehydrator

Both the liberally estimated plate and lodging unit are built of strong 304 evaluation tempered steel, and this huge business grade unit flaunts a completely computerized control board for included accommodation, with a 12-hour shutoff clock.

Situated at the higher finish of the value scale, it's for the idealist who acknowledges quality spotless materials, an extra-huge limit, and the force and solidness to run constantly.

A durable and trustworthy entertainer.

TRIBEST SEDONA

It is safe to say that you are searching for a propelled rack plate model that will perform to a more elevated level once it's completely stacked and all set?

On the higher finish of the value scale, the Tribest Sedona SD-P9000 offers a progressed, carefully controlled dehydration framework.

Tribest Sedona SD-P9000 Digitally Controlled Food Dehydrator

It flaunts a rich bundle with transparent glass entryway, and cases amazing execution because of its advanced getting dried out innovation, with exact temperature control.

It includes a straightforward, viable structure that makes activity simple, with plainly stamped controls and splendid LED advanced presentation on the front board.

Furthermore, the clock can be set for as long as 99 hours of effortless activity.

Nonetheless, the Sedona isn't without its issues – and they incorporate an inadequate degree of value control, and poor after deals administration. Regardless of its numerous appealing highlights, at the cost, you can improve.

Food dehydrators are easy to utilize, and the sound bites and fixings that they produce are incredible for weight watchers, and for spicing up your dinner times. I realize I was unable to manage without one in my kitchen.

HOW TO DEHYDRATE

If you've at any point felt the torment in your gut (and in your wallet) when you shell out for a solitary serve sack of dried extravagant mango, it's an ideal opportunity to roll out an improvement. Dried natural product is anything but difficult to make at home (all things considered, there's extremely only one fixing). Furthermore, truly, you do require an exceptional bit of hardware, as well.

There are a few different ways to get dried out natural product—you could depend on the microwave for firm organic product chips, or make chewy natural product calfskin in the stove—yet none is as idiot proof or as universally handy as utilizing the kitchen device made specifically for the assignment.

For the individual that depends on banana chips or dried mango cuts as a whenever (for example constantly) bite, and needs to go the hand crafted course, it's justified, despite all the trouble to put resources into a decent dehydrator so your wash room is constantly stuffed with a lot of fruity snack. Truly, you could utilize a broiler set at its least temperature, however most stoves run excessively hot to completely get dried out organic product without burning it.

Regardless of whether you're hoping to save your food, switch up your bite game or get ready for a future exploring trip, drying out your own food is simple and fulfilling. The drying procedure gradually evacuates dampness while holding supplements and flavor. Contrasted with prepackaged food, it tends to be less expensive and lighter as well, which is significant for explorers attempting to preserve space and cut down on weight.

Most got dried out food plans require a dehydrator, however there are a few things, similar to natural product cowhide, you can prepare utilizing a stove on a low setting. A mandoline slicer (utilized with alert) and a weight cooker can likewise speed the procedure up however aren't important to make flavorful dried out food. If you don't have a mandoline slicer, great knife aptitudes will prove to be useful.

Step by step instructions to choose a Food Dehydrator

Dehydrator with food covering the racks

Dehydrators commonly cost somewhere in the range of $30 to a few hundred dollars, contingent upon the measure of plate space and number of highlights.

If you're attempting to make a ton of food, it merits putting resources into a dehydrator with increasingly surface region because of the measure of time getting dried out takes (somewhere in the range of 5 to 14 hours). Square plate hold more than cycle ones with patterns in the center. A clock lets you go out without stressing over overdrying, yet is anything but a fundamental component. If you don't know what you need, start with a more affordable model, think about purchasing utilized or obtain one from a companion.

Two key highlights to search for are a fan for even warmth appropriation and numerous temperature settings to appropriately dry different kinds of food.

Nonstick sheets or material paper are required for drying sauces, soups and organic product cowhide. A few producers sell specific sheets that fit their dehydrator plate.

What Foods Can You Dehydrate?

Compartments of delightful looking got dried out food

Most food can be dried out at home, with the general rejection of dairy items and high-fat things. In contrast to organic produce, meat and most vegetables ought to be cooked first before getting dried out. When you have an assortment of dried fixings, you can collect them into dinners. Some entire dinners can be arranged and afterward got dried out, similar to soup and risotto. This limits prep significantly further and permits flavors to merge.

For proficiency, consider getting dried out an assortment of nourishments simultaneously, inasmuch as they require the equivalent drying temperature.

Food Prep: The Key to Dehydrating

Food shrivels significantly as it loses dampness, so remember that when thinking about the amount to make. For instance, a pound of apples (before cutting) yields about a cup of got dried out apple cuts. Albeit meagerly cut nourishments advance in any event, drying, don't cut pieces excessively little or they can lose all sense of direction in a supper when rehydrate.

Putting away Dehydrated Food

Zip-Lock packs of dried out food prepared for the path

The way to broadening the life of your food is forestalling oxidation.

Appropriately put away, evaporated organic product can last to five years and vegetables up to 10. If you will expend nonmeat things inside a year, keep them in cooler sacks or reusable stockpiling packs with the air crushed out. For long haul safeguarding, vacuum-fixing with an oxygen safeguard is ideal. Store in a cool, dull spot.

Meat and fish can be put away in cooler sacks and kept in a cool, dim spot if devoured inside a month; in any case vacuum-fixing and freezing is ideal. Meat put away appropriately in the cooler can keep going for as long as a year.

Utilize presence of mind—don't devour food that looks or scents malodorous.

Step by step instructions to Dehydrate Fruit

An apple and packs of dried out organic product

Organic product can be dried a couple of different ways: cut or mixed. Cut natural product makes an incredible nibble all alone, or it tends to be blended into oats or granola. Mixed, it dries into natural product cowhide that you can nibble on or rehydrate into pudding—especially if the mix incorporates bananas, which loan a rich consistency.

Organic product, regardless of whether cut or mixed, ought to be dried at 135°F until rough and malleable.

Apples in a Zip-Lock sack

2. Spot the apples in a bowl or plastic sack and include 1 tsp. of lemon juice and 1–2 tsp. of cinnamon, contingent upon your taste. If your apples are tart, include 1 tsp. of sugar (discretionary).

3. Mix well or shake sack to cover the apple cuts.

4. Spot on dehydrator plate and dry at 135°F for 8–12 hours until rough and malleable.

Step by step instructions to Dehydrate Vegetables

Bowl with got dried out vegetables

A general dependable guideline for drying out vegetables: If you can ordinarily eat them crude, you don't have to cook them before drying. Contingent upon your rehydrating strategy, however, you should cook every one of your vegetables first. If you plan to just add bubbling water to the food as opposed to heating up your supper for in any event a moment, steaming vegetables before drying makes them rehydrate better (perceive How to Rehydrate Dried Food underneath for additional subtleties).

To spare time, settle on solidified vegetables, which don't should be defrosted before going in your dehydrator. Canned vegetables are commonly too immersed to even think about drying admirably, except for beets.

Master tip: Don't get dried out onions—they make your entire house smell. Dried onions are moderately reasonable, and you can often discover them in the flavor area of your market.

Most vegetables can be dried at 125°F until dry. Some with higher dampness content, similar to zucchini and cucumber can be dried at 135°F.

Model Times and Yields

Solidified blended vegetables: Dry at 125°F for 6–8 hours; 1 lb. yields around 3/4 cup dry.

Mushrooms: Slice 1/8-in. thick and dry at 125°F for 6-8 hours; 1 lb. yields around 1/2 cup dry.

The most effective method to Dehydrate Meat and Seafood

Fish, from canned to dried out

Meat and fish are somewhat trickier than foods grown from the ground, as they should be warmed the perfect add up to eliminate microscopic organisms and once in a while need some support to rehydrate appropriately. You should just utilize lean meats, as fats and oils can go malodorous and ruin your food.

A wide range of meat ought to be dried at 145°F until hard and dry.

Meat and fish to consider:

Ground meat

Shop meats like lean ham, turkey and meal hamburger

Canned or pressure-cooked chicken

Canned fish

Cooked shrimp

Impersonation crab

Formula: Ground Beef

Pick lean or extra-lean meat just, as additional fat can prompt decay. Ground hamburger doesn't rehydrate well all alone; be that as it may, including bread pieces causes it assimilate enough dampness and gives flavoring. Include 1/2 cup bread scraps for each 1 lb. of meat. This will yield 2 cups of dry ground hamburger.

Crude ground hamburger in a bowl1. Put crude ground hamburger in a bowl and include bread scraps. Add salt and pepper to taste. Blend in with your hands until the morsels are uniformly disseminated.

2. Cook meat in a dish over medium-high warmth until gently seared and completely concocted, separating any huge clusters.

3. Spot meat on a plate with paper towels and smudge away any fat and overabundance dampness.

4. Spot nonstick sheets or material paper on plate to forestall losing little bits of meat. Spread the meat in a far, even layer.

5. Dry at 145°F for around 6 hours until meat is dim and dry, smudging any fat with paper towels and separating bunches a couple of times during the drying procedure.

Tearing open a bit of dried out meat

6. Tear open a couple of pieces to ensure they are dry completely through.

Formula: Chicken

Dried out chicken: Before and after

Home-cooked chicken won't rehydrate—it must be canned, or pressure cooked. White meat is better for drying, as it has a lower fat substance than dim meat. Notwithstanding adding chicken to dinners, you would cold be able to douse (add cold water to the sack) got dried out chicken for a couple of hours, channel the abundance fluid once it's rehydrated, and add mayonnaise and relish parcels to make chicken plate of mixed greens. A 12.5-oz. can will yield around 3/4 cup of dry chicken.

Chicken on plate for dehydrating1. Spread canned chicken uniformly onto plate fixed with nonstick sheets or material paper, separating any clusters. Smudge away any fat.

2. Dry at 145°F for around 8 hours until dry and weak.

Formula: Shrimp

Shrimp, prepared to get dried out

Pick medium-sized shrimp—little shrimp dry too little and bigger shrimp can set aside a long effort to dry. Precooked, solidified shrimp ought to be defrosted before drying. One lb. of shrimp yields 2 cups of dry shrimp.

Shrimp sets aside a more extended effort to rehydrate than most food, so let it presoak for a brief period longer before cooking.

Cut cooked shrimp into penny-sized pieces (around 4–5 for medium-sized shrimp).

Spread equally onto plate and dry at 145°F for around 6 hours.

Cut open two or three pieces to ensure they're totally dry inside.

The most effective method to Dehydrate Grains, Pasta and Legumes

Rice, quinoa, pasta and beans would all be able to be dried early and afterward fused into scrumptious suppers like chicken and veggie quinoa, bean soup, and spaghetti with meat sauce. Dried pasta likewise has the additional advantage of not waiting be depleted once cooked, as you can include sauce or potentially extra evaporated fixings to douse the overabundance water.

Cooking Tips: Grains, Pasta and Legumes

Cook rice and quinoa as you typically would (subbing stock for water adds season however make certain to utilize low or nonfat stock to help forestall ruining). Dry rice at 125°F for around 5 hours (or until hard) and quinoa at 135°F for 8–10 hours. Separate bunches varying. Two cups of cooked rice yield around 1/2 cups dry.

Cook pasta still somewhat firm and channel. For shorter noodles, spread uniformly on plate. For spaghetti noodles, twist a serving segment into a winding, home like shape. Dry at 135°F for 2–4 hours until hard.

Canned beans rehydrate obviously superior to home-cooked, except if you make them in a weight cooker. To dry, channel (and wash if canning fluid is extremely overwhelming) arranged beans and spread them in an even layer on plate. Dry at 125°F for 6–8 hours. A 15 oz. container of beans rehydrates to around 1 cup of dry beans.

You can likewise marinate noodles in soy sauce and different seasonings in the wake of cooking, and afterward get dried out them for a delectable Asian noodle plate of mixed greens with vegetables and shrimp. This can be cold-splashed for lunch—basically include a touch of cold water in the first part of the day, store the sack in a watertight spot, and by lunch your food will be prepared to eat.

The most effective method to Dehydrate Meals and Sauces

Dried out dinners

A few dinners can be set up to finishing before being dried out. Dishes like stews, bean stew and risotto all loan themselves well to drying.

Dried out Meal-Prep Tips:

Spread everything out daintily and equally, mixing on the plate now and then to guarantee careful drying.

Most dinners can be dried at 135°F for 8–10 hours. Simply ensure there's no outstanding dampness and separate bunches of food as it dries.

If the feast regularly incorporates cheddar, similar to risotto, include it independently subsequent to rehydrating.

The equivalent goes for sauces. Bumped or natively constructed tomato sauce can be spread onto nonstick sheets or material paper and made into tomato cowhide that will reconstitute with the expansion of high temp water.

Formula: Tomato Sauce

Tomato sauce being spread on a plate for dehydration1. Pick a sauce that doesn't have huge lumps of tomatoes or utilize a blender to puree. Maintain a strategic distance from gooey or rich sauces. Spread in a far, even layer on nonstick sheets or material paper.

2. Dry at 135°F for 6–8 hours, flipping at around 5 hours when you can without much of a stretch strip the cowhide off. (This is discretionary to make the drying procedure speed up, however the sauce will dry without flipping.)

3. The calfskin ought to be flexible and not clingy. Attack little pieces for simpler reconstituting.

Step by step instructions to Assemble Dehydrated Meals

Presently comes the great part—assembling your suppers. Get innovative and attempt different flavor mixes.

Balance your got dried out fixings with locally acquired things. For hiking trips, consider including things like powdered milk and sauces, bullion, moment pureed potatoes, flavors and cheddar. You can even convey oil in a crush container to include flavor and calories (a typical through explorer stunt).

Reusable capacity sacks and vacuum-fixed packs are ideal for holding single-serving dinners. Name the outside with the kind of dinner and the measure of water expected to rehydrate (most suppers require equivalent amounts of water to food). If the food is sharp, place a paper towel taken care of first to forestall punctures.

If there are fixings with higher dampness content, similar to organic product, place those in their own pack inside the principle dinner sack to get the dampness far from different fixings.

An ordinary supper serving is around 1 cup of dried out food. Increment to 1/2 cups for enormous segments.

Try not to restrain yourself to supper. Rehydrated natural product, joined with bread morsels, can be transformed into dessert. Quinoa with leafy foods makes for an incredible breakfast.

Look at our assortment of plans for motivation.

The most effective method to Rehydrate Dried Food

Dried out suppers for the most part require equivalent amounts of water to food and around 15–25 minutes to reconstitute. If you have one, a pot comfortable (a protected sleeve for your pot) holds heat while your food drenches.

Warming water to rehydrate food

Follow these means to prepare your supper:

Put food in pot and include an equivalent measure of water. Let drench for 5 minutes.

Heat water to the point of boiling. Turn heat down marginally and stew for 2–10 minutes.

Mood killer warmth and spread pot. Let sit for 10 minutes, or until food is delicate and completely rehydrated.

Include additional items, similar to cheddar, and appreciate.

Exploring professional tip: Take a little salt and pepper shaker intended for make a trip with you to modify seasonings on the path.

Two Recipes for Single-Serving Dehydrated Meals

Formula: Spaghetti and Meat Sauce

Fixings:

Capacity pack 1:

1 segment of dried pasta

1/4 cup dried ground hamburger (supplant with veggies for a vegan choice)

Capacity pack 2

1/4 cup pressed tomato calfskin

1/4 tsp. garlic powder

Parmesan cheddar as an afterthought

Headings:

Put noodles and hamburger into pot and simply spread with water. Let drench for 5 minutes.

Heat water to the point of boiling and include tomato cowhide. Stew and mix until tomato sauce reconstitutes.

Mood killer warmth, spread and let sit for an extra 5–10 minutes until meat is delicate. Add cheddar to wrap up.

Elements forgot dried out spaghetti and meat sauce

Formula: Shepherd's Pie

Fixings:

Capacity pack 1:

1/3 cup dried ground hamburger

1/3 cup dried blended vegetables (corn, carrots and peas)

1/2 bundle sauce blend

Capacity pack 2:

1/2 cup moment pureed potatoes

1/4 tsp. garlic powder

2 Tbsp. dried milk

Salt and pepper to taste

Cheddar as an afterthought

Headings:

Warmth 3/4 cup water in pot until bubbling. Fill sack with moment potatoes and manipulate pack to blend. Put in a safe spot.

Put meat, vegetables and sauce into pot and include around 3/4 cup water. Let douse for 5 minutes.

Heat water to the point of boiling and cook for 5 minutes. Mood killer warmth, spread and let sit for 5–10 additional minutes, until meat and vegetables are delicate.

Layer potatoes on meat and vegetables, including cheddar top.

HOW TO CHOOSE THE BEST FOODS FOR DEHYDRATION

Got dried out food is easy to make, delectable and an extraordinary method to cause your food to go that additional mile.

At Grundig, we have made the Respect Food crusade because we accept that your food merits a superior spot than the waste container. Food squander is a tremendous issue that influences we all. From landfills creeping higher and making destructive ozone harming substances, to the gap in our pockets getting further, it's an issue that we have to fix.

Regardless of whether you have a dehydrator, or regardless of whether you're utilizing a stove, these thoughts are a simple method to eliminate your food squander. Our inventive Respect Food advances make diminishing waste simpler. The Fast&Healthy broiler is exceptionally made to dry out your food while as yet keeping up its basic supplements. You can discover increasingly about a greater amount of our Respect Food innovations here.

Stuck for thoughts? Look at our rundown of nourishments that you can get dried out in your kitchen.

1. Meat

Make your own hamburger jerky! It's as basic as heating up your meat, blending sauce of your decision (garlic powder, onion powder, red pepper drops, salt and nectar function admirably), and covering the hamburger. Then, you should simply prepare it at a low temperature (about 80°C) for 3 to 4 hours, and you have your own custom made delicious hamburger jerky.

2. Bananas

Ever thought about how they make those delicious banana chips you get at stores? You don't need to sprinkle out to get them any longer; simply make your own from your extra overripe bananas! Cut the bananas, coat in lemon squeeze and prepare for around 3 hours at the most minimal temperature.

3. Vegetable Crisps

Add a sound bend to your preferred bite by utilizing your extra vegetables. Everybody adores crisps, yet these are crisps with a reason. In addition to the fact that they stop your veggies from winding up in the canister, but at the same time they're low in fat because they're got dried out, and not seared. Cut into uniform cuts, season and get dried out at the least temperature for around 4 hours. You can utilize any vegetables, for example, potatoes, turnips, mushrooms, kale, and even tomatoes.

4. Apples

Apples get an exceptional notice on this rundown because of how flexible they are. Make your dried out apples a sweet winter treat via flavoring them with some nectar, cinnamon and nutmeg, or give them a zesty kick with some bean stew powder and salt. Cut them into cuts, absorb water blended in with lemon juice (to forestall sautéing), season, and dry out for around 4 hours at 90°C.

5. Make some natural product calfskin

If your preferred natural product smoothie fixings are going off, include some lemon squeeze and nectar, mix them up, and afterward get dried out them. It's a delicious, solid tidbit to prop you up as the day progressed, made by sparing your natural product from winding up in the landfill. Spread the mixed natural product on a lined preparing sheet and get dried out at the most minimal temperature for around 6 hours.

6. Occasional natural products

Keep the late spring with you long after it's passed by getting dried out organic products, for example, melons and mangoes. Much the same as different nourishments on this rundown, the technique is straightforward: cut, season and get dried out at a low temperature.

Dried out nourishments can last you for a month or more (contingent upon the food) when put away in a hermetically sealed compartment in a cool, dull spot. Ideal for eating, lunchboxes and for in a hurry; got dried out nourishments are the adaptable method to lessen your food squander. Get dried out your food steadily and effectively with Grundig's Fast & Healthy innovation, and store your nourishment for longer with our HerbFresh, VitaminCare Zone and FullFresh+ refrigeration advances, which cautiously control air and temperature conditions in your ice chest.

DEHYDRATING AND STORING SAFELY

Drying is an incredible method to safeguard nourishments, yet just if you do it right. Here are a few hints to guarantee safe stockpiling of your home-dried nourishments:

Tips for Packaging Dehydrated Fruit and Dried Food

Try not to bundle dried nourishments for capacity until they are totally cool to the touch. The air encompassing the warm dried food will hold more dampness content, which is then discharged when it cools. You could wind up with beads of water in your capacity holder, which will decrease the time span of usability of the dried food.

Dried organic products must be adapted before they can be put away. You have to put them inexactly stuffed in containers. Shake the containers once per day for seven to 10 days. During the molding time frame, if you see buildup in the container, you ought to send the organic product back to the dehydrator for additional drying.

Store dried nourishments in hermetically sealed holders or cooler packs. You can utilize a container with a water/air proof seal, which can become stylistic layout just as capacity. If you utilize plastic sacks, they ought to be cooler packs, which are thicker than straightforward sandwich sacks.

If utilizing cooler sacks, make certain to expel all air from the pack before fixing.

Vacuum-fixing will give you the best timeframe of realistic usability as it evacuates air, getting dampness and form far from the dried food. It merits getting a vacuum sealer if you are going to dry food.

Store sulfured natural product in non-metal compartments or put it in a plastic pack before setting it in the metal holder. Something else, the sulfur will respond with the metal and can create off-flavors.

Store dried nourishments in little groups to keep up newness and to limit the danger of sullying. Putting away individual servings will guarantee you aren't opening and shutting the holder, acquainting air that can lead with trim and decay.

Mark every compartment with what it is and the date it was bundled. You would prefer not to have a lot of riddle things on your racks, and you will have the option to utilize the more established things before they start to lose their newness.

Tips for Storage of Dried Food

Store compartments in a cool, dry and dim area. A temperature of 60 F or 15 C (or less) is ideal. Introduction to light will corrupt dried nourishments, so if you store jolts out on your counter or retires, hope to utilize the food in the near future.

Dried vegetables and meats can be hidden away as long as a half year.

Store dried nourishments in the cooler if you'd prefer to utilize them over a more drawn out timeframe.

If buildup shows up inside one of the holders of your home-dried food, it should be dried once more.

Store things so the more seasoned things are in front or on top so you can go through them while they are still of acceptable quality.

Tips for Using Stored Dehydrated Fruit and Foods

To safeguard newness, store opened holders of dried nourishments in the fridge or cooler.

Assess every single dried food before eating them, and dispose of anything with form. If in question, toss it out.

Drying out food goes past the pragmatic side of loading your wash room with nutritious, delectable nourishments; you increase individual fulfillment realizing that you made this put away abundance with your own hands. You'll feel a feeling of pride and freedom, cultivating an association with ages before who utilized these food dehydration standards.

Getting dried out organic product requires an extraordinary advance called "molding," a procedure that evens out the dampness, because all the natural product pieces probably won't have dried similarly because of their size or position in the dehydrator. After the dried organic product has cooled, pack it freely in a glass container. Seal the container, and let it sit for 10 days, shaking the container day by day to isolate the pieces. The overabundance dampness of some organic product pieces will be consumed by drier natural product pieces, restraining mold development. Vegetables for the most part don't should be adapted, because they as of now are extremely dry when they've completed the process of getting dried out.

When completely dry, pack the got dried out food in perfect, dry, bug confirmation and dampness safe holders, for example, glass containers, metal jars and plastic cooler compartments or sacks. Ensure the holder has a tight-fitting top. Pack got dried out food in modest quantities, because each time a compartment is revived, the food is presented to dampness and air that cause decay and influence food quality. When opening a holder for utilization, completely examine the got dried out food. Dispose of it promptly if there are any indications of form or waste.

Store dried food in a cool, dry, dim territory; higher temperatures cause shorter capacity lengths. Dried food commonly can be put away for one year at 60 degrees F yet for just a half year at 80 degrees F. Dried vegetables ordinarily have a large portion of the timeframe of realistic usability of dried organic products. For best flavor and expanded timeframe of realistic usability, freeze or refrigerate dried jerky.

"Safeguarding food, by any strategy, permits us to eat and appreciate the kinds of summer during winter and late-winter months when our nurseries are resting or not yet in full creation," says Melinda Hemmelgarn, a Missouri-based enrolled dietitian, editorialist and radio host. "With any technique for food conservation, the objective is to save exactly what you'll require until the following developing season. Take notes. Did you come up short on canned tomatoes, natural product cowhides and solidified berries a year ago? Continuously plan your nursery, gather and conservation techniques as needs be."

PRO-DEHYDRATING TIPS

Avocados have high oil content and therefore are not suggested for dehydration. They won't store well and will turn smelly after a timeframe.

Fundamental tips before you start

Here are some extra tips:

Wash Everything Down: Use an enemy of bacterial chemical of your decision. Much the same as when canning nourishments, it is essential to rehearse great cleanliness while drying out too. This guarantees a decent final result with a more extended timeframe of realistic usability.

Wear Latex or Vinyl Gloves: There is regular oil and dampness in your grasp, which will defile your nourishments by reintroducing dampness. Modest "expendable" gloves like these are advantageous, however you can likewise reuse them so they will last more!

Warm Up Your Dehydrator: Air dissemination helps for an equally dried item and takes out the development of sullies, therefore it is ideal to begin the dehydrator and get the air going before presenting your food

Attempt Scissors: It is a lot simpler to cut dried out nourishments with kitchen scissors than a knife! Some got dried out nourishments you can just disintegrate in your grasp.

Utilize Stainless Steel: If you utilize a knife that isn't tempered steel to cut certain things, for example, bananas, the last item will seem browner in shading. These are still fine to eat, just less engaging.

Whitening and skin singing

Whitening is when you place your food in bubbling water for around 30-60 seconds before drying out.

For what reason do you need to steam or whiten a few things and not others?

Skin singing happens during the whitening procedure. Skin singing is done to soften the skin of an organic product or vegetable to help the break of dampness, or help the evacuation of the skin. While whitening a grape, for instance, you should whiten it before getting dried out so as to soften the skin for better dampness expulsion. While whitening a tomato or peach, be that as it may, you whiten to take into account simple skin expulsion: you will discover they simply fall directly off!

Food that ought to be whitened or skin singed:

Grapes

Tomatoes

Blueberries

Plums

Fruits

Peaches

Cranberries

Pears

Summer squash

Zucchini

Getting dried out Blueberry tips

Spot blueberries in a pot of bubbling water for around one moment. Next, add cold water to the bubbling pot, then spot the dehydrator plate over the sink and pour on the blueberries, similar to a sifter. The less you need to move them around the better. Next, the mystery is to prick each berry with a toothpick to allow the air to out. Dry out at 125°F. for around 18 hours. If a few blueberries are still enormous and delicate, they are not completely dried out. Cut another gap in those ones, and spot again into the dehydrator for 3-6 for quite a long time.

Will you over dry your food?

No, you can't over dry. Rather, the genuine concern ought to be under drying, as leaving dampness in your food can make it ruin. Be that as it may, if you expel 95% or a greater amount of the dampness from your food and store appropriately your food will keep going for a considerable length of time and taste extraordinary. Therefore, if you are uncertain if your food is dry, keeping it in the dehydrator longer won't hurt.

Case Hardening

Case solidifying happens when the temperature is excessively high, making the food solidify outwardly and the dampness to stay within. When this happens the dampness will ruin the foods after some time, and it should be discarded. You will realize you have case solidifying from the appearance; the external instance of the food will be clear, and within will be dim or dark.

Keeping away from case solidifying is an unquestionable requirement for fruitful long haul stockpiling. Many individuals suggest 135°F for products of the soil for vegetables when drying out. It has been our experience that 120-125°F. is the best temperature for the two leafy foods. Longer time with lower temperature is the best technique to forestall case solidifying. If you get case solidifying, take a stab at getting dried out at a lower temperature for a more extended span whenever.

Would you be able to fix case solidifying?

If you have case solidifying you now and again can turn it around. To do this, cut the pieces down the middle or put a cut in the highest point of the food and set back in the dehydrator, this permits the caught dampness to get away. For cut potatoes, essentially jab them with a sharp knife and spot them again into the dehydrator. Little cubed potatoes are too difficult to even consider correcting, so just cook them and eat them before they ruin. They are still acceptable to eat you simply would prefer not to store them long haul.

Cheddar, milk, margarine, eggs

Cheddar, milk, eggs, and margarine should be monetarily handled with unique hardware. Things with high oil content should likewise be handled utilizing unique business techniques and will turn rotten in a brief timeframe if done mistakenly. It has been suggested by specialists in food stockpiling and getting dried out that these things be bought through an organization that can monetarily process such things.

Eggs, be that as it may, can be mixed and got dried out and afterward rehydrated with bubbling water, yet you can't utilize these dried out fried eggs in cakes, breads, or other heated merchandise. The time span of usability when done at home isn't as long as though bought by an organization. Dried out scramble eggs are extraordinary for climbing or outdoors. My recommendation is to purchase powdered eggs that have been securely dried out by business hardware and appropriately put away. They taste extraordinary (like a new egg), and are increasingly flexible for cooking, and are protected. The equivalent goes for cheddar, margarine and milk.

Picking flour

Entire Wheat Berries: This flour can be put away for 30+ years in the berry structure if held in an impenetrable holder with a decent elastic seal and a 2000cc oxygen pack for every 5-gallon volume of wheat. In any case, when ground, entire wheat flour ought to be put away in the cooler or cooler in an impermeable compartment until it is prepared to utilize. "Hard" berries, for example, hard red winter, hard white winter, hard white spring, or hard red spring demonstrate that it is wheat with a high protein level (14%). This wheat is incredible for breads. In any case, delicate wheat, for example, generally useful flour and cake flour contains less protein (10-12%) and is incredible for cakes and baked goods.

Unbleached Flour: Flour that is brightened utilizing oxygen (has a greater amount of a grayish appearance).

Faded Flour: Flour that is handled with chlorine. The chlorine, be that as it may, dissipates in the wake of handling. Handling the flour lessens sullying and improves the time span of usability (2-5 years if put away appropriately). Dyed and unbleached flour are practically the equivalent.

Advanced Flour: Flour that is enhanced with iron and four B Vitamins (thiamin, niacin, riboflavin and folic corrosive) to supplant what was expelled from the grain and germ. Also, calcium is enhanced. There is no adjustment in taste, shading, surface, preparing quality, or caloric estimation of the enhanced flour.

Pre-Sifted Flour: Flour that is sifted at the plant, making it superfluous to sift before estimating. In any case, when your flour is vacuum stuffed and put away for an extensive stretch of time it is consistently a smart thought to sift it once more, in any case if it had been sifted already.

Entire Grain Flour: Flour that contains the germ, grain, and endosperm of the wheat bit. Diets wealthy in entire grains decrease the dangers of heftiness, diabetes and heart conditions.

Cake Flour: This flour is lower in protein, lighter, fluffier, and is utilized for cakes, baked goods, and biscuits. Practically all cake flour is dyed. Fade toughens the particles permitting the flour to convey more sugar and fat. This flour can be bought in the heat products segment of your market. Or then again, you can set up your own by taking 1 cup of generally useful flour and evacuating 2 tablespoons of the flour and supplanting it with 2 tablespoons of cornstarch. If you need it to act naturally raising then include a touch of salt and 1 ½ teaspoons of heating powder to the blend. Record these estimations and tape it to the rear of your flour canister.

Natural Flour: This flour is sans compound. It is developed and put away without the utilization of manufactured herbicides or bug sprays. It likewise implies that no poisonous fumigants were utilized to murder bothers in the grain and no additives were added to the flour, bundling or food item. Natural flour, in any case, isn't normalized, so its definition shifts from state to state.

Cooking with dried beans

Dried beans are extraordinary to use in your pre-bundled nourishments. Dinners containing dried beans should be set up with a moderate cooker (slow cooker). This is because beans take any longer than noodles or grain to rehydrate and cook. I suggest utilizing a simmering pot with all soups. The cook time is around 5 1/2 hours or longer with a stewing pot. Obviously, with dried beans it will take longer, and it is consistently a smart thought to drench them before cooking.

Dehydration versus Awful Bacteria

A portion of the principle debasing specialists that cause your food to ruin after some time are microscopic organisms, form, and parasites. Besides, certain food contaminants can be hazardous to wellbeing, causing food contamination and different sickness. When putting away food, therefore, it is imperative to be learned of these contaminants so as to expand the timeframe of realistic usability of food, and secure your wellbeing. You will be glad to discover that appropriate food dehydration for all intents and purposes kills the dangers from injurious contaminants. How? Fundamentally through the special blend of these three variables!

Temperature: As expected, most microbes that are pathogenic to people flourish at human internal heat level (98.6 °F). When the temperature starts to transcend that temperature the development of numerous microbes starts to slow, and some incredible;

the adequacy of having a fever when you are wiped out! Some regular hurtful food borne microscopic organisms incorporate Clostridium botulinum (botulism), (salmonella food contamination), and pathogenic Campylobacter or E. coli (food contamination). The development of almost all strains of these unsafe microscopic organisms eases back somewhere in the range of 98.6 and 112 °F or higher. Dehydration is normally performed at 120-125°F for most things, with the exception of when getting dried out meat where higher temperatures are utilized (155-160°F).

Evacuation of Air: Some pathogenic microscopic organisms are high-impact (flourish within the sight of oxygen), and some are commit aerobes (will pass on without oxygen). All things considered, air evacuation through vacuum fixing murders or represses the development of some pathogenic microorganisms. Besides, an appropriately fixed vacuum sack will keep new microscopic organisms from arriving on and colonizing your food.

Evacuation of Moisture: The most significant obstruction to the development of contaminants is the expulsion of water. If performed appropriately, dehydration should evacuate in any event 95% of dampness, leaving 5% or less dampness content. Most microorganisms, form, and parasites can't develop, and often pass on, beneath 10% water content. Food stockpiling methods, for example, freezing and canning, where the food is as yet liable to water, represent an expanded hazard for food sicknesses if not performed appropriately.

As should be obvious, the regular bacterial reasons for food disease are not a significant reason for worry with food dehydration. The danger of bacterial tainting in appropriately dried out nourishments is amazingly low, and is lower than canning and freezing, making it the most secure food stockpiling strategy for the three. Truth be told, the most elevated hazard for pollution of your got dried out nourishments is really creepy crawlies! To forestall this, just ensure the entirety of your food things are in fixed vacuum packs, Mylar sacks, or containers, and that your capacity sacks are not punctured.

Despite the fact that the danger of foodborne ailment coming about because of got dried out nourishments is very low, it is as yet essential to rehearse legitimate cleanliness and sterile procedure. It is ideal to remain erring on the side of caution and forestall any presentation of defilement when conceivable. Sterile procedure is basic. Wash all things with cleanser and water, or flush with water, before getting dried out. Ensure all kitchen surfaces and utensils are spotless. Wearing latex or vinyl gloves will likewise help keep the presentation of oils from your hands into your nourishments.

Dehydrators: Which one to pick?

When purchasing a dehydrator the most significant thing to search for is the fan situation. The fan ought to be situated on the rear of the dehydrator NOT on the top or base. Dehydrators that are structured with a fan on top or base will dry your food unevenly along these lines making confounding drying times and poor air flow. Additionally if the fan is on the base flavors from nourishments on your base rack will go into food sources on higher racks, making undesirable flavors.

I suggest Excalibur Dehydrators. I at present have two 9 plate Excalibur Dehydrators. One was bought in 2007, and the other in 2009. Neither has given me a solitary issue and the two of them run continually day and night and give fabulous looking items. These are by a long shot the best dehydrators I have ever utilized. To guarantee devotion from my watchers I ONLY suggest items or administrations I have by and by utilized and feel are the best accessible for the expense.

Drying times

It is difficult to give a specific time period for drying out nourishments because of the considerable number of factors included. Moistness outside and in the home, thickness and sort of cut, how stacked the plate are, and even different brands of produce have a major impact in dehydration time. Additionally, the sort of dehydrator you use assumes a huge job. If the fan is on the top or base of your dehydrator it will take more time for the food to dry because the dissemination of wind stream is upset by different plate. If the fan is in the rear of the dehydrator (like these models) your food will dry quicker and all the more uniformly.

What I can let you know is this:

You never need to expand the temperature to dry food quicker, as this will build the danger of "case solidifying." This is when the outside of the food solidifies and dampness is caught within. This will make your food ruin. By and large, the best drying strategy is "longer time, lower temp". Never attempt to speed things up by expanding the temperature. Notwithstanding if I am drying out an organic product or vegetable, I once in a while go over 125°F.

Average* Drying Time List

8-15 hours All new vegetables including peppers

8-10 hours Frozen vegetables (make sure to put on the plate while solidified)

8-10 hours Mushrooms and onions (cut and cleaved)

12-15 hours Sweet and white potatoes (slight cut, slashed)

8-10 hours Fruits if cut extremely flimsy

12-15 hours Fruits if cut in ¼ inch cuts

15 hours in addition to Fruit rollups (contingent upon how much corn syrup and nectar utilized)

15-20 hours Grapes

18-20 hours Blueberries

As long as 2 days Whole prunes (evacuate pits)

12-15 hours Peaches, plums, pears, apples, nectarines, rhubarb

* "Normal" times are given since dehydration time can be modified marginally by a variety of factors including dampness, kind of dehydrator, and thickness of your food. The most significant part isn't so much the period of time in the dehydrator, however the level of residual dampness left in your food. For long haul stockpiling you need to remain at 95% or more. Testing for dryness will be your best gauge. Your food ought to effortlessly snap and ought not be staying together.

Professional Tip: After getting dried out your food, place it in a zip lock pack for a couple of days before putting away in your vacuum sacks. This will allow you to see that your food has completely dried out. If your food seems limp you can return it in the dehydrator again for a couple of more hours.

Nourishments that ought to be steamed before getting dried out

ALL LOW ACID FOODS:

Beets

Corn

Carrots

Asparagus

Cabbage

Peas

Beans

Broccoli

Potatoes

Cauliflower

Green Bean

Pumpkin

Peas

Nourishments requiring no prep

The accompanying nourishments you basically cut and toss on your dehydrator; no pre-treatment of any sort is required (for example no whitening, lemon juice, steaming, and so forth.)

Oranges

Lemons

Limes

Collard Greens

Spinach

Mushrooms (If wet or absorbed water before getting dried out mushrooms will turn dull in shading. These are still OK to eat)

Parsley

Dill

All herbs

Step by step instructions to Dehydrate Frozen products of the soil

Remember that you can dry out the entirety of your solidified foods grown from the ground from your market, sparing you room in your cooler. All your solidified nourishments have just been prepared, simply open the sack and toss them on the plate solidified. This incorporates thick French fries and hash earthy colors. Melons are better if pureed and made into organic product rollups. Solidified strawberries are simpler to cut when they are just mostly solidified.

Organic product move up tips

Never use sugar in natural product roll-ups, the sugar will take shape after some time. Rather utilize nectar or corn syrup.

When utilizing zip lock packs to dry your organic product roll-ups, ensure any print on the sack is confronting ceaselessly from the move up.

Use pipe tape to tape down the zip lock sack so it doesn't tumble off in the dehydrator and it is anything but difficult to expel from the plate.

Psychologist wrap makes an incredible bundle for the roll-ups when fixed utilizing your sealer.

Additionally, the wax embeds in grain boxes make an extraordinary bundle for organic product roll-ups.

Cooking the organic product in a pot before drying out makes the move up translucent, though uncooked makes for an all the more firm and strong shading move up.

Natural product Skins

Spare the strips when stripping oranges, mangos, papayas, apples, peaches, pears, and lemons. Spot the skins on the plate with the skin's external surface looking DOWN and get dried out. In the wake of getting dried out, most skins can be ground and placed in natively constructed home grown teas, sauces, treats, cakes, and breads.

Natural product tips

When all is said in done, most organic products can be got dried out at 120-125°F. The occasions for getting dried out natural products go contingent upon the organic product, and how thick you cut them. Likewise, different organic products some of the time require different preparing techniques preceding drying out.

Essential Fruits:

Most natural products ought to be dried out 8-10 hours if cut extremely slim, or 12-15 hours if cut around 1/4 inch thick. Thicker cuts will expand the time further.

Preceding dehydration most organic products require preparing. Often this involves basically cutting them to a uniform thickness, spreading them on the dehydrator plate, and splashing them with lemon juice. Citrus and other high-corrosive natural products are readied a similar way, aside from without splashing with lemon juice.

FRUIT RECIPES

Chicken with Dried Plums and Sage

Yield

4 servings (serving size: 1 chicken bosom half and around 1/2 cup sauce)

Fixings

4 (6-ounce) skinless, boneless chicken bosom parts 2 tablespoons slashed new wise, partitioned 1/2 teaspoon salt 1/4 teaspoon dark pepper, separated 4 teaspoons olive oil, isolated 2 cups meagerly cut onion (around 1 enormous) 1/2 cup dry white wine 1/2 cup without fat, less-sodium chicken stock 12 pitted dried plums, divided 1/2 teaspoons balsamic vinegar

Step by step instructions to Make It

Stage 1

Spot every chicken bosom half between 2 sheets of rock solid cling wrap; pound to 1/2-inch thickness utilizing a meat hammer or little overwhelming skillet. Sprinkle chicken with 1 tablespoon wise, salt, and 1/8 teaspoon pepper.

Stage 2

Warmth 2 teaspoons oil in a huge nonstick skillet over medium warmth. Add chicken to skillet; cook 3 minutes on each side or until done. Expel chicken from container; keep warm. Warmth staying 2 teaspoons oil in container. Add onion to dish; cook 3 minutes or until delicate. Mix in wine and stock; heat to the point of boiling. Include staying 1 tablespoon savvy and dried plums to skillet; cook 4 minutes or until blend thickens. Mix in staying 1/8 teaspoon pepper and vinegar.

Softened Plums with Vanilla Yogurt

The perfect summer pastry is new, succulent, not excessively sweet, and not excessively confused, which is the reason this finish of-season treat includes just six fixings. Skip turning on the broiler by cooking the plums just on the oven. The plums cook sufficiently long to often marginally and discharge their juices; utilize a knife and fork to make a plunge. Margarine, nectar, and squeezed orange blended in with juice from the peaches makes a light syrup that is just celestial. Sub any toasted nut or seed for the granola. This formula serves four individuals, and each segment of three peach parts

114

bested with yogurt and the peach syrup contains only 25g of included sugar, 184 calories, and 6.6g of fat.

Preferable and simpler over a plum fresh, skip turning on the broiler by cooking the plums just on the oven. The perfect summer pastry is new, succulent, not excessively sweet, and not excessively muddled, which is the reason this finish of-season treat includes just 6 fixings. The plums cook sufficiently long to soften somewhat and discharge their juices; utilize a knife and fork to make a plunge. Sub any toasted nut or seed for the granola.

Fixings

2 tablespoons unsalted margarine 1/2 tablespoons nectar 6 medium ready plums, divided and pitted 3 tablespoons new squeezed orange 1/2 cup vanilla 2% decreased fat Greek yogurt 1/4 cup low-fat granola

Step by step instructions to Make It

Stage 1

Join spread and nectar in a huge nonstick skillet over medium; cook until margarine dissolves. Add plums to container, chop sides down; cook 8 to 10 minutes or until softly seared and delicate. Partition plums equitably among 4 serving bowls or glasses.

Stage 2

Add squeezed orange to skillet; cook over medium 3 minutes or until somewhat thickened, mixing every now and again. Expel dish from heat.

Stage 3

Top each presenting with yogurt and granola; sprinkle uniformly with juice blend. Serve right away.

Melon and Prosciutto Salad with Parmigiano-Reggiano

Salty and unctuous, prosciutto is a great counterpart for new melon, and a garnish of Parmigiano-Reggiano (the genuine stuff is justified, despite all the trouble here) includes another layer of exquisite flavor. Make this serving of mixed greens the focal point of a simple appetizer supper. Present with a platter of olives, broiled peppers, cut tomatoes, mozzarella cheddar, and, if you're feeling goal-oriented, include your preferred flame broiled or simmered veggies, as well.

Yield

8 servings (serving size: around 3/4 cup)

This beautiful hors d'oeuvre formula would be a fine expansion to an appetizer spread. Parmigiano-Reggiano gives nutty differentiation to sweet melons and mirrors the flavor of salty prosciutto.

Fixings

3 cups (1/2-inch) cubed honeydew melon (around 1/2 medium melon) 3 cups (1/2-inch) cubed melon (around 1 medium melon) 2 tablespoons daintily cut new mint 1 teaspoon new lemon juice 1/4 teaspoon newly ground dark pepper 2 ounces meagerly cut prosciutto, cut into slight strips 1/2 cup (2 ounces) shaved new Parmigiano-Reggiano cheddar Cracked dark pepper (discretionary) Mint twigs (discretionary)

Step by step instructions to Make It

Stage 1

Join initial 5 fixings, hurling tenderly. Mastermind melon blend on a serving platter. Mastermind prosciutto uniformly over melon blend; sprinkle with Parmigiano-Reggiano. Enhancement with split dark pepper and new mint twigs, if wanted.

Stage 2

Wine note: I worship the sweet-salty-natural kind of this serving of mixed greens. It's so reviving thus summery. A decent wine accomplice ought to radiate similar attributes. While you could settle on an Italian pinot grigio, I locate a more full bodied California pinot grigio works far better, particularly given the full kinds of the prosciutto, mint, and Parmigiano. An incredible decision: Estancia Pinot Grigio 2005 (California), $ - Karen MacNeil

VEGETABLE RECIPES

Firm Liempo Sinigang Rice Recipe

Firm Liempo Sinigang Rice with Vegetable Tempura is my interpretation of soup-less sinigang. It has a similar decent and asim-kilig sinigang flavor, with an incredible sauce you will enjoy.

Talong At Fish Torta

Talong at Tuna Torta is a sort of eggplant omelet (or tortang talong). A bit of eggplant was bubbled until delicate, and plunged in beaten egg before the consumption.

Shrimp Laing Formula

This shrimp laing formula is my adaptation of the famous vegetable dish that began from the Bicol area.

Pork Munggo With Kangkong Formula

Pork Monggo with Kangkong is a simple to-make variant of ginisang monggo. It utilizes extra lechon kawali and water spinach.

Ginataang Langka With Dilis

I appreciate eating ginataang langka since I was a child. Everything began when I attempted a comparative dish at my folks' old neighborhood in Romblon.

Kalabasa And Corned Hamburger Pieces Formula

Kalabasa and Corned Beef Nuggets can be a decent option in contrast to chicken tenders, only for a change. This formula is basic and direct.

Ginisang Repolyo At Giniling With Oyuster Sauce Recipe

Ginisang Pechay at Giniling with Oyster Sauce is a speedy and simple dish to cook during occupied days. It just takes under 30 minutes to get ready, it is less stressful and unique.

The most effective method to Cook Kilawing Labanos

Kilawin is equivalent to ceviche. It is the Filipino method of getting ready food by marinating in corrosive. Fish, meat, and vegetable can be marinated.

Ginataang Bitsuelas

Ginataang Bitsuelas is a Filipino vegetable dish wherein green beans are cooked in coconut milk. I additionally include a touch of pork into the formula to give it a nourishing taste.

Ginisang Togue

Ginisang Togue is essentially Sauteed Mung Bean Sprout with carrots, chime pepper, shrimp, and tofu. This Mung Bean Sprout formula is a customary dish.

MEAT RECIPES

Pork Tenderloin with Balsamic Onion-Fig Relish

Caramelized onion and figs draw out the common pleasantness in pork here. Attempt the relish with chicken or hamburger too.

Wash room Checklist:

Pork tenderloin (1 lb)

Dried Mission figs

Balsamic vinegar

Low-sodium soy sauce

Onion

Prep: 4 minutes

Cook: 10 minutes

Other: 5 minutes

Skirt Steak with Corn and Red Pepper Puree

Red Bell Pepper gets utilized two scrumptious ways: as a vegetable in the corn sauté and as a pureed sauce for the plate. New corn isn't simply sweet; it has an astonishing hit of umami force.

Wash room Checklist

Fish Sauce

Red Bell Pepper

Green Onions

Skirt Steak

Corn Kernels

Hands-on: 30 minutes

Absolute: 60 minutes, 30 minutes

Orange-Balsamic Lamb Chops

A basic citrus marinade in addition to a brisk burn yields significantly more flavor than you might suspect. Obviously, a completing balsamic sprinkle is consistently welcome.

Wash room Checklist

Olive Oil

Ground Orange Rind

Squeezed orange

Sheep Rib Chops

Balsamic Vinegar

Flame broiled Steak with Pineapple Rice

With only five fixings, this protein-stuffed dinner meets up instantly. Soy sauce amps up the kind of meat tenderloin filets, which pineapple loans tropical flavor to brown rice.

Wash room Checklist

Lower-Sodium Soy Sauce

Meat Tenderloin Filets

Can Pineapple Slices in Juice

Green Onions

2 Packages Precooked Brown Rice

Meat Tenderloin Steaks with Red Wine-Mushroom Sauce

Mushrooms include an appetizing flavor that makes hamburger taste much meatier, while red wine brings corrosiveness for balance. Rampage spends on extraordinary steaks in this straightforward formula; with not many fixings, the meat radiates through.

Storeroom Checklist:

Hamburger tenderloin steaks (4-4oz)

Infant portobello mushrooms

Red wine

Margarine

New rosemary

Prep: 1 moment

Cook: 10 minutes

Sweet-Spiced Grilled Lamb Chops

There's no explanation sheep shouldn't be a standard piece of your menu arranging with a dish as straightforward and heavenly as this. It coordinates well with any kind of arranged grain: grain, couscous, quinoa, or even corn meal.

Storeroom Checklist:

Sheep flank hacks (8-4 oz)

Ground cinnamon

Ground allspice

Ground cumin

Ground red pepper

Prep: 2 minutes

Cook: 6 minutes

Slow-Cooker Beef Pot Roast

Nothing beats pot broil for a delightful supper on a cool day, and the moderate cooker makes this formula for all intents and purposes easy. Extras for sandwiches are an absolute necessity doesn't as well, stress if this appears to be a great deal of meat.

Wash room Checklist:

Boneless shoulder pot broils (2-lbs)

Mushrooms

Chime pepper

Ketchup

Worcestershire sauce

Prep: 4 minutes

Cook: 7 hours and 7 minutes

Stuffed Cuban Pork Tenderloin

While the pork is cooking, add new vegetables to the flame broil for a total supper.

Wash room Checklist:

Bread-and-Butter Pickles

Dijon Mustard

Pork Tenderloin

Cilantro

Swiss Cheese

Pork Medallions with Spicy Pomegranate-Blueberry Reduction

Cutting pork tenderloin lets it cook through quickly and makes this dish superfast; the sweet-fiery sauce of natural product juice and chipotle chiles makes it interesting.

Wash room Checklist:

Pork tenderloin (1 lb)

Garlic powder

Solidified pomegranate-blueberry juice condensed

Chipotle chiles, canned in adobo sauce

Prep: 2 minutes

Cook: 11 minutes

CONCLUSION

Before placing the food into the food dehydrator, consistently cut them into one-fourth inch pieces or areas. This will permit the ideal introduction of the surface to the warmth and wind stream of the dehydrator.

However much as could reasonably be expected, equitably convey the cuts of food over the dehydrator sheets. This will likewise encourage the way toward drying, making it extremely broad and compelling.

It is fitting to inconsistently examine the drying state of the food. The things which are situated close to the aficionado of the food dehydrator will dry out quicker than different nourishments. This can be helped by then again repositioning the plate following a few hours.

Make a point to painstakingly dry out food and give them an opportunity to chill off at room temperature before setting them inside a compartment which has a water/air proof seal. Regardless of whether the dampness level of food expelled from the dehydrator is at a low level, they can even now discharge some measure of water. The dampness will be kept out of the water/air proof holder if the food is given a chill off period directly after it experiences dehydration and before putting them inside the sealed shut compartment.

Irregularly perfect the dehydrator utilizing lukewarm water especially close to the base of the dehydrator where little bits of food may have gathered.

Evaluate an assortment of food things, plans and the different strategies for getting ready food.

Never endeavor to quick track the drying procedure of the food by expanding the temperature of the dehydrator over the recommended temperature level that the food should be presented to. If this is done, solidifying will happen or a fractional dehydration will happen and the food will have a hard surface with within still soggy which will ruin the food things too soon.

Dry out food things of a similar kind together. Dry out vegetables along with different vegetables and natural products with different organic products. Try not to dry out asparagus or onions along with bananas and different sorts of natural product.

Continuously mark the holders of the dried food with the date when they were dried out. You will have the option to screen the age of the food things and its time span of usability with this.

CPSIA information can be obtained
at www.ICGtesting.com
Printed in the USA
BVHW041646131020
590917BV00007BA/58